D1268129

**CONTEMPORARY** WRITERS IN CHRISTIAN PERSPECTIVE
A CONTINUING SERIES EDITED BY RODERICK JELLEMA

# Charles Williams

A CRITICAL ESSAY BY
MARY McDERMOTT SHIDELER

WILLIAM B. EERDMANS/PUBLISHER

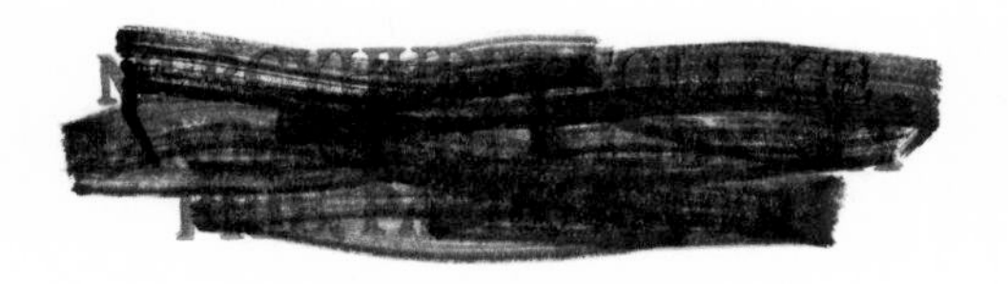

Library of Congress Catalog Card Number, 66-22955
Printed in the United States of America

# CONTENTS

# I

# THE MAN AND HIS WORK

BETWEEN 1912 AND 1946, THE LITERARY AND THEOLOGICAL worlds were enlivened by the appearance of forty-odd books, several hundred poems, plays, articles, and reviews, and one short story, by Charles Walter Stansby Williams, an editor in the London office of the Oxford University Press. Then and since, some people have been moved by his work into words of rhapsodic praise. Others have been repelled by it to the point where language could scarcely express their aversion. Still others have read one or two of his books and found themselves unable either to comprehend what he was saying or to forget the disturbance he had awakened within them. Time and again I have mentioned his name in casual conversations, only to have someone turn immediately and say, "I once read something by him. For heaven's sake, what was he talking about?"

The violence of the reaction to Charles Williams' work can be documented from critical articles and reviews. An unidentified reviewer of *He Came Down from Heaven* declared in an English periodical that "Mr. Williams's book is probably one of the most remarkable (not for its size, not 'of its kind,' not at its price, but absolutely) of our generation". H. D. Hanshell commented, "Williams was a critic, novelist, poet, playwright, and theologian (of a sort), and all to a greater or lesser extent manqué. He had a liveliness of mind and energy, but his famed 'originality' was basically a matter of indiscipline of spirit." Geoffrey Parsons wrote that Williams' novels "contain some of the noblest and most moving pages in English literature," and that *Descent into Hell*, specifically, has "a climax that has few parallels in any art outside, perhaps, the glory of a great cathedral." In the judgement of F. R. Leavis, "Williams's preoccupation with the 'horror of evil', is evidence of an arrest at the school-boy (and -girl) stage rather than of spiritual maturity". John Press gave his opinion that Williams' poetry is "uncouth and rebarbative", and described him as "a very queer fish in a deep, dark pond". And C. S. Lewis, evaluating Williams' later poems, stated that "they seem to me, both for the soaring and gorgeous novelty of their technique and for their profound wisdom, to be among the two or three most valuable books of verse produced in the century".

Nothing in Williams' biography would lead one to expect from him a body of work that evokes such controversy. His life exhibited no dramatic episodes or radical conversions. He was a Londoner by birth, and a lover of cities who regarded even Oxford as a "provincial centre". Except for a brief period at the beginning of his career, he spent all his working life with the Oxford University Press. An Anglican by heritage and upbringing, he remained always a devoted member of that church. And he was happily married and the father of one child, a son.

Charles Williams was born in 1886, the son of a shopkeeper, and died in 1945. Being educated at St. Albans Grammar School in the later years of Queen Victoria's reign, he received a straightforwardly classical education, which terminated during his first year at the University of London when his family could no longer support him there. During World War I, he was barred from military service for medical reasons, and he seems to have taken no part in the activities from which the "Flaming Twenties" received their name. Then and in the early 1930's, he was active in the burgeoning adult education movement, lecturing at evening institutes established primarily for workingmen, of whom he once said to a conference of academicians and ecclesiastics, "These are the people who are capable of re-energizing your culture. . . . They are, much more than your more academic students, a centre of power".

When the Second World War began, the offices of the Oxford University Press were moved to Oxford where Williams already had friends, among them an informal group called

"The Inklings", whose members included C. S. Lewis, J. R. R. Tolkien, Dorothy L. Sayers, W. H. Lewis, Fr. Gervase Mathew, and Owen Barfield. During this period, the University of Oxford awarded Williams an honorary M.A., and appointed him as lecturer in English literature. It was in Oxford, shortly after VE Day, that he died, and it is in "provincial" Oxford that he is buried.

The impression given by this catalogue of events is dull. Yet the picture conveyed by those who knew him is that of an extraordinarily vital man, "tall, slim, and straight as a boy".

> His face we thought ugly [wrote C. S. Lewis]: I am not sure that the word 'monkey' has not been murmured in this context. But the moment he spoke it became, as was also said, like the face of an angel — not a feminine angel in the debased tradition of some religious art, but a masculine angel, a spirit burning with intelligence and charity.

And his conversation was "a continual flow of gaiety, enthusiasm, and high spirits". Many of his friends have reported on the range and depth of his friendships. W. H. Auden has written that "in his company one felt twice as intelligent and infinitely nicer than, out of it, one knew oneself to be", and C. S. Lewis, that when Williams was absent, his friends felt that "some principle of liveliness and cohesion had been withdrawn from the whole party: lacking him, we did not completely possess one another".

This radiance, however, had not been easily achieved, nor was it easily maintained. In his life as in his writing, Williams showed himself to be profoundly oppressed by the agonies and tragedies of human existence, its confusions and uncertainties, and the monotonies that dog all our ways. This was no mere matter of an alternation in moods. It reflected his considered judgement that the contradictory extremes of our lives are inextricably bound together. "Good contains terror," he wrote in his novel *Descent into Hell*. In another novel, *The Place of the Lion,* he showed the perception of ultimate beauty as fatal. In his essay "The Cross", he pointed out that "the supreme error of earthly justice" — the crucifixion of Jesus — "was the supreme assertion of the possibility of justice": man rightly condemned the God who, having created the kind of a world we have, is responsible for the horrors we endure, and God confirmed the justice of our accusation when he submitted to it and suffered in himself what he allows his creatures to suffer.

The theme of the active union, the co-inherence, of great opposite experiences and ideas pervades all Williams' writings. His most masterly exposition of it is in the cycle of poems in which he retells the Arthurian legend. Here also the complexity, subtlety, and richness of his thought finds its most adequate expression in a superbly complex, subtle, and rich poetic style. These poems have a further importance in that Williams thought of himself as primarily a poet, and only secondarily a novelist, essayist, theologian, editor, or critic. There is little doubt that his poetry will be long studied and loved, but "poet" defines the style, not the content, of a writer's work, and in the words of his close friend Anne Ridler, "the ideas he was expressing were always more important to Charles Williams than the medium of expression". Now, he is most widely known for his seven novels: "supernatural shockers" they have been called, in which enthralling adventure stories become vehicles to convey provocative insights into the nature of the world and of man. For example, a priest in an obscure village parish discovers that the Holy Grail is sitting in a cupboard in his church. A sophisticated young woman converses face to face with a man who had died several hundred years earlier. A Lord Chief Justice of England is instantly transported across London merely by holding a certain stone in his hand and wishing to be elsewhere. Of course such things are impossible — or are they? The same themes reverberate in his theological studies and critical works. There are indeed things in our midst that are authentically holy. Separation in time does not prevent the exchange of love. Distance in space is not an insuperable barrier to personal interaction.

The disputes over Charles Williams' work arise principally from his world view and his understanding of the nature of man, and the main portion of this brief study will be devoted to them. As a preliminary, however, something needs to be said about his literary style. Its most striking feature is probably its constant changes of pace. Here he lingers over an idea, stating and restating it in a variety of ways. There he packs profundities into an adjective. Again he darts backward or forward or to one side, tracing an implication. This movement of thought gives even to his prose something of the quality of what Gerard Manley Hopkins called "sprung rhythm", with concepts juxtaposed almost as if they were sounds, so that it is not only his words that dance together, but his ideas. Because of this tumbling flow of thought, none of his books can be grasped at first reading, any more than a great symphony at first hearing. The later passages illuminate and fulfil the earlier ones, so that until one knows how the first statement of the theme is resolved, he cannot apprehend it properly. Therefore the best way to read anything that Williams wrote is first to skim it in order to see his whole pattern, and only then settle down to a careful reading.

Neither can one be sure, on first meeting Williams' work, what he meant by certain terms that are common currency of speech, but that frequently are defined so loosely that they no longer convey any depth of meaning or force. He was an implacable enemy of cant, and "he used words as poets do; he regenerated them" by employing them with precision. While this does not make his books easier to understand, it does charge them with great power. And he is fair to his readers: he always makes clear what he means by such words. A quotation from *He Came Down from Heaven* will demonstrate both the process and the effect: "The famous saying 'God is love', it is generally assumed, means that God is like our immediate emotional indulgence, and not that our meaning of love ought to have something of the 'otherness' and terror of God."

It is worth noting that here, as with other words, he does not radically alter the ordinary and older meanings, but clarifies and heightens them. The vague connotations are not destroyed but made explicit. Any careful reader will, in any case, submit himself to what he is reading while he is reading it, however he may dissociate himself from it when he has finished. Because of these redefinitions, he may find such submission more difficult with Williams than with other writers. Or he may find it easier, as Williams gives substantial meaning to ideas toward which he has long been groping, and finds himself at home in the world that Williams displays before him.

In several important respects, the world of which Williams writes is markedly different from that which most of us have been trained from childhood to see around us. Therefore, he is presenting not simply an assortment of new ideas which can be fitted into the framework of our ordinary thinking, but another framework, another arrangement for all our ideas. The contrast between these two world views is easier to perceive than to analyze, not because Williams is at all unclear, but because any pattern of thought that pervades a culture contains so many variations that it is exceedingly difficult to pin it down, even by such broad labels as "secular materialistic humanism". Moreover, Williams spent considerably less of his energy in directly attacking his opponents than in exhibiting his alternative.

His major themes appear in every aspect of his work. Somewhat — but not altogether — arbitrarily, I have chosen to use his novels as the medium for examining his interpretation of the world, his Arthurian poems for showing how he understands who and what man is, his plays for the consideration of the ultimates of life, and his non-fiction as the basis for a concluding — but not conclusive — estimate.

# II

# THE WORLD IN THE NOVELS

CHARLES WILLIAMS' SECOND NOVEL, *War in Heaven,* WRITTEN in 1926, exhibits with particular simplicity and directness the contrast between his world view and that which is currently predominant in much of Western civilization. The central character in the book is an Anglican archdeacon, rector of the English village church of Fardles, "a round dapper little cleric in gaiters" who has the pleasant habit of singing psalms half-aloud as he goes about his errands, and who maintains his sedate common sense even in the face of an imminent and singularly horrible destruction. Upon him converge three sets of events and characters. The body of a murdered man is found under a desk in an office of a respectable London publishing firm. One of its editors shows the Archdeacon page proofs of a book which says that the Holy Grail is probably in the Fardles church. And the author of the book attempts first to buy and then to steal the chalice, in order to use it for sorcery. The plot develops in the form of two interlocking chains: a detective story, with the search for the identity of the murdered man and for the murderer; and an adventure story, with the Grail in the possession now of one party and now of the other.

Corresponding to these two strands of the plot are the two types of power which the characters employ: the natural powers of bodies, minds, and machines — all the physical, social, and psychological energies that are available in nature and can be used for good or evil; and the divine and demonic powers of supernature that are imaged by the Holy Grail and by witchcraft. The latter are not, however, such supernatural agencies as are characteristic of popular belief and disbelief. Williams is not predicating two separate but overlapping worlds, but a single world, a *uni*verse, in which things that we know by our senses and reason are continuously interacting with things that we know by other ways.

> The use of the word supernatural has been rebuked [he wrote in his history of witchcraft], and indeed it is a little unfortunate. It did not imply then [the first century A.D.], nor should it ever have implied since, any derogation from the natural order. But it did imply that that order was part of and reposed on a substance which was invisible and which operated by laws greater than, if not in opposition to, those which were apparent in the visible world.

Thus the relation between nature and supernature is so close that a deliberately evil act, such as the wanton murder in *War in Heaven,* taps supernatural energies that pull the murderer down into even uglier iniquities, and a redemptive act, like the Archdeacon's offering of himself in the service of the Grail, is sustained both by the potency of the holy thing and by the unobtrusive activities of the polite young man in grey, carrying gloves and a cane, who is the supernatural Priest-King, the Keeper of the Grail.

The very idea of supernature sounds preposterous to a world that has come by unheeded steps to identify the statement, "Here is the domain of scientific and rational investigation" with "Here is the domain of reality and truth". The habits of a lifetime and the basic structure of nearly all our thought impel us so strongly into dismissing supernaturalism as such, that it requires constant and sometimes strenuous effort to break away from this negative credulity, although it is as blindly prejudicial as the most naive superstitions about ghosts and fortune-tellers. Most of us carelessly define "spirit" and supernature as entities or functions that are not physical, intellectual, or emotional, and either reject them out of hand as fantasies, or treat them with inexcusable sentimentality and lack of intelligence.

By contrast, the Archdeacon and his adversaries are operating from the closely reasoned conviction that the powers of the universe may become incarnate in many ways, from Brownian movement and the ebb and flow of the sea to the Eucharist and the Black Mass, and they see all these powers as sharing the same fundamental nature and therefore as capable of effectively interacting. To them, it is no more surprising that the Grail can be disintegrated by willing its annihilation than that the intention of a husband and wife to separate should dissolve a marriage, or an acid neutralize a base. Still exercising disciplined intelligence, they do not suppose that such operations as the attack on the Grail by the prayer of conjuration or its defence by the prayer of invocation can succeed without at least as much prior knowledge, skill, and practical training as is required — let us say — to fly a weather observation plane into and out of the eye of a hurricane.

The title *War in Heaven,* therefore, does not refer to a conflict between nature and supernature, but to the involvement of the divine and the demonic in all our affairs, no matter how mundane or sublime. Forces that are authentically supernatural play upon natural events, and the life of the spirit is conceived of as being as real, as potent, and fundamentally as natural, as the ordinary material and mental functions of our ordinary existence. All creatures are moving toward order or chaos, co-inherence or incoherence, and whichever way we take, we have access to the supernatural and it has access to us.

This is decidedly not, for Williams, a matter of spiritualism or of collating the form and content of prayers with the events that follow their utterance. In his judgement, such activities are silly and dangerous: silly for the same reason that it would be silly to use a thermometer for measuring wind-velocity — the instrument is inappropriate to the purpose; and dangerous because supernatural forces are greater than any natural energies, and the laws of supernature are so little understood that our ignorance may easily lead to our destruction. Its ways are not our ways, and if there is any such thing as supernature, we are probably happier and assuredly safer if we leave it alone.

But it does not leave us alone. Many of us, at some time or other and in some form or other, have been visited by the irresistible sense of the Other, indescribable and heavy with ecstasy or dread, and by this invasion of our complacencies we have known, in astonishment, that we were confronting something or someone infinitely different from ourselves. This experience can be attributed to any of a number of sources, but in the end, the interpretation we place upon it will be determined by whether we have decided to assert that Nature — everything that has temporal or spatial existence, including our mental processes — is ultimate and autonomous, or whether we have decided instead that Nature is derived from and continuously subject to beings or forces that are not limited to time, space, and thought.

How can we determine conclusively which of these is in fact true? We cannot. As the Archdeacon replied when he was asked whether the cup at Fardles was actually the Grail, "No-one can possibly do more than decide what to believe," and this is as true of the scientist — who decides to believe his sense experiences, his premises, his instruments, his procedures, his colleagues, and his own sense of the fitness of things — as it is of the poet, the metaphysician, the mystic, the logician, and the ignorant.

In his first novel, *Shadows of Ecstasy* (1925), Williams states unambiguously what he himself had decided to believe. His protagonist here is Sir Bernard Travers, at the moment when he is contemplating the infatuation of his son Philip for a girl named Rosamond. While Sir Bernard is fully aware of Rosamond's mediocrity of mind and character, he does not conclude from this either that Philip is a blind fool, or that Rosamond is unworthy of Philip's adoration. The commonplace girl seems divine to her lover? Very well:

> A thing that seemed had at least the truth of its seeming. Sir Bernard's mind refused to allow it more but it also refused to allow it less. It was for each man to determine how urgent the truth of each seeming was. . . . A thing might not be true because it appeared so to him, but it was no less likely to be true because everyone else denied it. The eyes of Rosamond might or might not hold the secret origin of day and night, but if they apparently did then they apparently did, and it would be silly to deny it and equally silly not to relish it.

An astronomer would rightly disclaim that Rosamond's eyes have anything to do with the onset of daylight and dark, but the fact that Philip feels this way conveys directly something important about her, as well as indirectly something important about him. The beauty that is born in the eye of the beholder is conceived by an impregnation from a source outside that eye. Some quality in Rosamond herself evoked his response from Philip, and nothing in anyone else had the capacity to wake him in this fashion and depth. Since most of her friends found no unusual grace in her, the conclusion might be drawn that she was not, in reality, what Philip thought she was. According to Williams, however, it would be more accurate to say simply that her appearance to them contradicted her appearance to Philip. And it would be more just to ascribe equal reality — or unreality — to both appearances, while of necessity determining for oneself which appearance shall direct one's own relationship to her.

Returning to *War in Heaven,* this same principle governs the answer to the question, "Is this the Grail?" It would be flagrantly credulous to declare that because it seems to be, it is. But it would also be credulous to deny it on no ground other than the *a priori* belief that the Grail does not or cannot exist. Because the appearances conflict, investigation is called for from both sides. "The distinction between necessary belief and unnecessary credulity is . . . the heightening and purifying of belief", and the casual or contemptuous rejection of an appearance because it contradicts what we believe to be the underlying reality, is as gravely damaging as the frivolous neglect of a reality in favor of its appearance. And there is nothing in the universe that can save us from the necessity and the responsibility for deciding which of these we shall adopt for our own.

It is not necessary to agree with Charles Williams on supernaturalism in order to comprehend or enjoy his work. It is necessary to realize that he meant what he was saying when he proposed that what we call *"this* world" is not a closed system, but an open one. What it opens upon is a manner of living in which even time and space become subordinate to loving and being loved, knowing and being known, so that by actions in time and space, we can transcend those limits. Williams' most dramatic account of this process occurs in his next to last novel, *Descent into Hell* (1937), which some critics consider his finest.

Its setting is Battle Hill, a prosperous suburb of London. Its time is the indefinite present. A group in this community plans to produce a new play written by the pre-eminent English poet of the period, Peter Stanhope, who is a resident of the Hill and has agreed to help with the production. One of the young women in the cast, Pauline Anstruther, attracts Stanhope's attention because she seems to live in a state of perpetual anxiety. At his urging, she explains that off and on for years, she has seen herself approaching her on the street — not another person whom she mistakes for herself, and not a hallucination, but her own self: the *doppelgänger*. And she is certain that someday she will meet this other self face to face, and will then die or go mad. Meanwhile, her grandmother, Margaret Anstruther, is slowly and serenely dying. A nameless man who had committed suicide some years earlier goes wandering about the Hill, seen only by Margaret and (finally) Pauline. And the Hill's other internationally famous inhabitant, the historian Lawrence Wentworth, pursues his solitary quest for happiness, which culminates in his descent into hell.

The method by which Wentworth reaches damnation is simplicity itself. When Adela, the woman he desires, jilts him in favor of a younger suitor, he rejects the painful fact and consoles himself with an imaginary mistress who has Adela's form and voice but is utterly pliant to all his desires. When another historian is awarded an honor he had coveted, he persuades himself that it was a political appointment. Aflame with resentment against these personal and professional humiliations, he withdraws into himself to the point where he will not trouble to mention a minor error in the costuming of the play when he is called upon for an expert opinion, even though its correction would require no effort from him and little from anyone else. In these and other ways, he cuts himself off from friendship and scholarship, from all the acts of giving and receiving by which biological and personal life are supported and increased, until while still outwardly a living man, he dwells in a timeless solitude without memory and with no perception except that of the interminable, impenetrable monotony of negation.

At the other extreme are Stanhope the poet and Margaret the dying woman, who between them introduce Pauline to the way of exchange — the ways of giving and receiving that fulfil and transcend nature. Stanhope, discovering Pauline's fear of meeting herself, reminds her that the confrontation might be pleasant rather than disastrous if she were not afraid of it, and he offers to carry her fear for her, as if a burden of terror (or pain or remorse or grief) could be transferred like a bag of groceries from one person to another. "It's a fact of experience," he tells her. "If you give a weight to me, you can't be carrying it yourself; all I'm asking you to do is to notice that blazing truth." He goes on to say that such an exchange is not only practicable, but required by the nature of things.

> If you insist on making a universe for yourself . . . if you want to live in pride and division and anger, you can. But if you will be part of the best of us, and live and laugh and be ashamed with us, then you must . . . give your burden up to someone else, and you must carry someone else's burden. I haven't made the universe and it isn't my fault. But I'm sure that this is a law of the universe.

Reluctantly, incredulously, Pauline agrees to let Stanhope carry her fear for her and he takes it up, enduring in her stead the panic of her anticipation.

This form of what Williams called "substituted love" is basically natural rather than supernatural, although he shows the potentialities of nature as being rather more extensive than most of us have been led to expect. There are a variety of hypotheses from psychology, psychiatry, and other disciplines to explain the manner of its operation, or to explain the phenomenon away until the thing that seems true — that the burden actually is carried by someone else — no longer is permitted even the truth of its seeming. And if we apply psychological categories of explanation to the event, we shall assuredly produce explanations that are psychological in character. But if we begin where Williams did, with the apparently real event (and while no doubt the incident is fictitious, there is also no doubt that Williams was describing a process in which he and others have participated) — if we begin with the event, stripping ourselves temporarily of our habitual cynicism, we shall discover what Pauline did when she found that she was no longer afraid.

> A violent convulsion of the laws of the universe took place in her mind; if this was one of the laws, the universe might be better or worse, but it was certainly quite different from anything she had ever supposed it to be. It was a place whose very fundamentals she had suddenly discovered to be changed.

More changes await her. Having been initiated into the acts of substituted love by giving Stanhope her burden, she is offered the opportunity to bear a burden for another. The appeal for her help comes to her from one of her ancestors, who had been martyred four centuries earlier. She can answer it because she is living in the present, and the time in which he had lived had been the present for him. In the infinite contemporaneity which is eternity, all "present" moments co-inhere, so Pauline can meet her ancestor and carry his fear, and in this act her meeting with herself finally takes place.

If we have never done any such thing, it is possibly because it has never occurred to us to try. Or if the technique has been brought to our attention, it may have seemed so strange that we have scoffed at the idea and discarded it. "There is always a necessity for intelligence," Williams remarks dryly in the midst of his theological analysis of substitution in *He Came Down from Heaven,* but by intelligence he means something other than the detached, rational intellect. The attempt of the philosopher to attain coherence of ideas is a noble enterprise, but Williams is concerned with a greater one: to see and live in the co-inherence of all things, personal and spiritual as well as intellectual, and historical as well as philosophical and scientific. It is important for man to be logical, but it is imperative for him to be integrated, to order not only his mind but also his life.

Unquestionably, an ordered life is impossible without ordered thought, but a supremely well-organized system of ideas can co-exist with a chaotic personal life and lead to a tragically divided existence. In recent years, such concepts as "the feeling intellect", "the logic of the intellectual heart", and "those terrifying syllogisms . . . which are as much of the blood as of the brain", have received more attention from artists than from scholars, to the detriment of both. These, however, represent the realm within which Charles Williams chose to operate, and his supernaturalism has its roots in this soil.

Recent developments in the analysis of language and of thought-processes have led us to become suspicious of philosophical and theological system-building, "philosophies of life", and world views such as Williams' own. That he was also skeptical of their value is attested by his statement, written in 1933:

> But patterns [of thought] are baleful things, and more so because the irony of the universe has ensured that any pattern invented by man shall find an infinite number of facts to support it.

Therefore it is futile and absurd to search the cosmos for universal principles and a coherent synthesis. But also, as Williams clearly understood, the processes of philosophical, theological, and aesthetic analysis are equally futile and absurd.

The recognition of these absurdities has produced in some philosophers and artists a soul-racking nausea. For Williams, on the contrary, they were a source of continuing delight. He wrote of the "excellent absurdity" that enables us to discern how "Poetry is a good game — let us take it lightly. But it is also 'liberty and power' — let us take it seriously". And "There is nothing that matters of which it is not sometimes desirable to feel: 'This does not matter'." But to understand why this absurdity should exist at all, and how it can properly be called "excellent", it is necessary to turn to his interpretation of human love and divine judgement, especially as they are expressed in the cycle of Arthurian poems which he did not live to complete, and in his major plays.

# III

# THE POETRY OF LOVE

INSTEAD OF TAKING KING ARTHUR OR LANCELOT OR GALAHAD as his protagonist in retelling "the Matter of Britain", Charles Williams chose a more obscure figure of the legend: the king's poet Taliessin, who as a child had been found floating in a coracle down the River Wye, and was adopted by a tribe of pagan Welshmen. They nurtured him to manhood when, hearing tales of the City and Empire of Byzantium, he set forth to find them.

> Dim and far came the myth to Taliessin
> over the dark rim of the southern sea.
> Poor, goetic or theurgic, the former spells
> seemed beside the promise of greater formulae;

poor — control or compact — the personal mastery,
the act of magic, or the strain of ancient verse
beside the thickening dreams of the impersonal Empire

. . . . . . . . . . . . .

His heart turned to know more than could be learned
by Wye of that white healing metaphysic;
he sought the sea and the City; he was caught by a rumour.

The poems are not presented as a continuous narrative, but like the earliest sources of the Arthurian legend, by means of incidents whose sequence and interconnections are not spelled out. The first dozen poems of this cycle were published in the privately printed *Heroes and Kings* (1930) and interspersed in *Three Plays* (1931). In them, as in his four earlier volumes of poetry, Williams was feeling his way into the material and working out the style which he brought fully under control only in the course of writing the thirty-two poems of *Taliessin through Logres* (1938) and *The Region of the Summer Stars* (1944). He wrote of the first poems that they belonged to "an attempted and unfinished cycle . . . which proposed to begin with the distress of Logres [Arthur's Britain], to speak of the vision of the elect soul, of the establishment of Arthur, of the transmutation of the Table at the coming of the High Prince [Galahad], and of his achievement. Outside which (as some tell us) man has no concern".

The proposition that the quest of the Grail is or ought to be man's sole concern requires immediate attention. We are right in asking what we have to do with this mythical kingdom and its inhabitants, or with any myths, we who are so harried by brutal facts. It can justifiably be said that the Round Table and the Grail are not living symbols for persons who from childhood have been immunized against all myth and fantasy, and who have never believed in the holiness of the Holy Grail if they have heard of it at all. Surely these stories are dead; they do not speak in our tongue or to our condition.

This may be true. Or it may be that it is we who are dead. It sometimes seems that our ears are open only to what we call "realism" or "naturalism", and are closed to the austere voice of the classical mood and the ringing tones of romanticism. It has become commonplace to identify the reality of love with sex, and the reality of sex with its messier physiological concomitants. It is fashionable to celebrate society and the individual in jargon or broken phrases, avoiding even the cadences of consecutive speech, and to employ the crudest verbal expressions that we can find. Such treatment of the matter and form of human life is entirely legitimate in itself, and valuable as a reaction against the classical and romantic excesses of the past. It is not the error of this fashion but its tyranny that is damning, not the insistence that this harsh word be cried aloud but the demand that no other shall be heard, as if an individual could not or should not be stirred by the paintings of both Jackson Pollock and Andrew Wyeth, or as if a love for Mozart's music were to preclude the enjoyment of Ives'.

The legends of King Arthur and of the Grail, singly and in their fusion, are obviously not "realism" in the sense that critics usually employ the word, but they are centrally concerned with the question, "What is real?" Many of the writers who are currently most conspicuous are tacitly defining reality in terms of what the eye can see, the hand can touch, and the ear can hear. The classicists have always dealt with reality in terms of the ordering and clarifying functions of the disciplined mind, and the romantics in terms of the overwhelming personal experience of rapture or outrage. Charles Williams has distinct affinities with all of these tendencies. C. S. Lewis wrote that

> he starts from the very depth of the romantic tradition and, without ceasing to be romantic, advances to the acceptance of all that is at first sight furthest from romanticism. In him the poetic tradition which had begun in Pantheism, antinomianism, and revolt, ends in Nicene theology, moral severity, and the celebration of order.

But Williams' method of using symbols has contributed to obscuring his realism and classicism, not because it is inherently peculiar or difficult, but because few of us have been trained to recognize and use it.

Williams was not an allegorist as, for example, was John Bunyan, whose Christian cannot be made to symbolize Everyman or any man, but only Christian man. He was an imagist like Dante, whose actual Beatrice was a symbol of many things besides salvation, and could have been used to symbolize an indefinite number of other things, some of them inimical to salvation. A convenient illustration of the distinction between allegory and imagery — which is vital for reading Williams' poetry and novels — comes from the opening verse of Psalm 19, "The heavens declare the glory of God", which can be read either way.

To begin with allegory: the psalmist may have wished to communicate an idea of God's glory that was already reasonably clear to him, and looking around, decided that this concept could be expressed better by comparing it with the heavens than with the ocean, the mountains, the birth-death-rebirth cycle of nature, or the splendor of the human heart. To enhance the poetic effect, he may have turned the literally exact but passive statement, "The glory of God is like the heavens", into the figurative but active, "The heavens declare the glory of God". If he functioned in this manner (and we have no way of knowing whether he did), using the heavens, the law, and other aspects of the world as *convenient illustrations,* he was an allegorist. Many people do habitually think in this manner, and apparently it is their natural mode of thought.

On the other hand, the psalmist may have looked at the heavens and discovered that they revealed to him something he did not already know about the divine glory, so that his line was a literal description of his experience. If he observed the world in this way, with the things and activities around him serving as *instruments for discovery,* he was an imagist, and in company with many others to whom imagery is a natural mode of thinking and perceiving.

The method of imagery is closely associated with what has been called in another connection "the scandal of particularity": the declaration — immeasurably shocking to the fastidious rational mind — that persons and events which in themselves are local, immediate, and material can reveal transcendent glories and convey that glory into the most ordinary aspects of our lives. Thus Dante's Beatrice can image salvation because she is known as her own self; it is the maculate girl who communicates the immaculate glory. Similarly, for Williams

Taliessin is an image, not an allegorical representation of "the poet in his relation to society and God". He is explicitly a unique person, confronting situations and problems that are strictly his own and that would be unusual in any social or spiritual setting. It is because he is himself that he can illuminate for us the character of our own and others' uniqueness. And because his story is set in a definite historical period (although Williams knowingly allowed some anachronisms), we gain through him a sharper sense of our own movements through our own history. The very differences that mark his and our individualities are means by which we discover our identity with him.

The supreme examples of imagery for Williams were the human body as it images the human spirit, and human love as it images divine love. He writes that the boy Taliessin "grew and practised verse; / striving in his young body with the double living / of the breath in the lung and the sung breath in the brain", the internal rhyme reinforcing Williams' thesis that physical and poetic development are two varieties of one process, two categories of one identity. In a later poem, he is even more explicit in his identification: "Flesh knows what spirit knows, but spirit knows it knows", and "Flesh tells what spirit tells (but spirit knows it tells)". Still another example will suggest the subtlety and complexity of which imagery is capable. While Taliessin, "in a passion of patience", is watching the Battle of Mount Badon and waiting for the critical moment to attack the enemy's flank, he reflects that this attitude of intense, unhurried expectation is identical with that of a poet — Virgil, for instance — who delays in setting down a word until he has found the one that is needed. And as Taliessin envisions Virgil finding and writing the word, he sees the signal from King Arthur for him to charge.

> In the silence of a distance, clear to the king's poet's sight,
> Virgil was standing on a trellised path by the sea.
> Taliessin saw him negligently leaning; he felt
> the deep breath dragging the depth of all dimension,
> as the Roman sought for the word, sought for his thought.
>
> . . . . . . . . . . . . . .
>
> Civilized centuries away, the Roman moved.
> Taliessin saw the flash of his style

dash at the wax; he saw the hexameter spring
and the king's sword swing; he saw, in the long field,
the point where the pirate chaos might suddenly yield,
the place for the law of grace to strike.
He stood in his stirrups; he stretched his hand;
he fetched the pen of his spear from its bearer;
his staff behind signed to their men.

As patience is always patience, whatever the circumstances in which it is exercised, so — Williams declares — love is love whether it occurs between God and man, or between men and women. Human love is not "suggestively similar" to divine love; the two have real identity. This is not to say that they are identical, but to maintain that the single reality can be expressed in two — or many — styles, as an idea can be expressed in poetry or prose, spoken or written words, or gestures or demonstrations. The central question for every man is what his real identity shall be: love, or hate or fear or detachment or any of the other possibilities. His second question is what style he shall use to express his identity: marriage or celibacy, politics or poetry, romanticism, classicism, or realism, and so on.

Since Williams' major theme in these poems is the identity of love, it is especially important to follow Taliessin in his achievement of it. His journey from Britain to the City of Love, Byzantium, takes him along the road between Logres, the historical kingdom torn by internecine warfare, and the supernatural forest of Broceliande, where he feels "the power of universal spirit rise / against him to be wild and savage on his lonely spirit". When he reaches Byzantium, he finds it a place where "the streets repeat the sound of the Throne". Here history and eternity, nature and supernatural grace, are integrated. It is a closely structured and finely ordered society, its citizens as diverse in structure and function as the parts of the human body, yet as precisely co-ordinated as a geometrical diagram. The City is, in fact, an incarnation of its Emperor, such an incarnation as Britain is meant to be in its own style, and as Rome and Gaul and Jerusalem are meant to be in their styles. And when Taliessin leaves Byzantium, it is not merely to carry back to Britain this vision of an ordered passion (and contrary to common belief, an ordered passion is not a contradiction in terms), but also to be himself the seed that will impregnate Britain with its reality.

The grand design of establishing the Byzantine order of love fails for Logres as a whole, but it succeeds in limited ways, thereby ensuring that it will not be forgotten in times to come, but will retain its power to enliven the minds and imaginations of future generations. Galahad achieves the Grail, and Taliessin's household gathers around him. The rule of this household is what Williams calls "the law of exchange". At its elementary, natural level, this means the giving and receiving of "labour in the kingdom, devotion in the Church", and the glad acceptance of "the need each had of the other". At the second level are those who bear one another's burdens, "according to the grace of the Spirit / 'dying each other's life, living each other's death' ". At the third level are those few slaves and lords, priests and mechanics, who are aware that the human interchanges are images of the reciprocal love among the Persons of the Trinity.

All life is predicated upon giving and receiving, from the physical interplay of sub-nuclear particles and the biological processes of ingesting and egesting, to intellectual and personal development. We can resent the necessity for exchange, or we can embrace it and willingly develop its arts and skills, growing in grace and truth and building the City of Love. In this activity, the Christian has an added power because he performs consciously and deliberately the acts which all men, willy-nilly, must perform if they are to live at all. For example, because man is a social being, he is constantly being assailed by new ideas, and he can receive them grudgingly because he cannot avoid them, or sensibly concede them as opportunities to increase his knowledge, or welcome them with joy as occasions for participating more fully in the infinite web of exchange.

The ordering of the exchanges which characterizes Byzantium and Taliessin's household stands in sharp contrast to the two other kinds of order that are shown in Williams' Arthuriad. One of these is imaged by the Saracen knight Palomides, and the other by the Empire of P'o-L'u. In Islam, the exchanges are curtailed by "the sharp curved line of the Prophet's blade / that cuts the Obedience from the Obeyed". Allah commands and his worshipper submits, but the cleavage between them is absolute, because Islam repudiates the doctrine of incarnation — not only Jesus as the incarnation of God, but the principle that the divine being can be incarnate at all. Therefore, in Islam there is no claim that in their various degrees, human loves image and incarnate the love of God. Nor is there any exchange of function, such as in the Christian belief that the God to whom man must submit has in turn submitted himself to man, in Jesus' trial and crucifixion and all the other acts where man exercises his freedom in disobedience. Lacking the incarnation, Islam images for Williams something else as well: that spiritualizing of religion which he sees as a cardinal sin, and in which, for example, sexual interplay is construed as a religious rite instead of being enjoyed for its own honest sake, and sexual abstinence is interpreted as a suppression of man's "lower nature" instead of as one of the means for expressing the integrity of man. "The maxim for any love affair is 'Play and pray; but on the whole do not pray when you are playing and do not play when you are praying.' We cannot yet manage such simultaneities."

In Williams' thought, as in orthodox Christian theology, Islam is a heresy. But P'o-L'u is hell, the opposite of Byzantium. Its ideal life is one of utter monotony; its acts are directed to the annihilation of exchange; and its headless Emperor walks, clothed in a crimson cope, accompanied by octopuses. This state of being is what Mordred — King Arthur's son by his incestuous union with Morgause — craves for himself. Conceived by a sexual exchange in which, as C. S. Lewis wrote, "the strain gives itself not to another strain but only back to itself", Mordred deliberately perpetuates and intensifies that introversion.

> He sought his vision by mere derision of the vision.
> He drew into the ordained place of the Table
> the unstable pagan chiefs; all personal
> griefs in Logres burst and curst the impersonal
> formulae of glory; he assuaged his own image
> with the image of the Throne, setting both against the Empire,
> and begetting by the succubus of his longing, in a world of pagans,
> the falsity of all images and their incoherence.

In brief, Mordred rejects the City of Love; Palomides perverts it; and Taliessin fulfils it.

It is significant that in telling the story of Taliessin, Williams shows him as seeking and finding Byzantium before he meets and falls in love with the Princess Dindrane. Personal love is among the most important exchanges of life; as Williams says in his treatise on Dante, Beatrice — the beloved — "is an illumination by grace", through whom the lover sees the vision of Very Love. But, he goes on, "one could do without Beatrice; one cannot do without the City". The point of glory within the web of exchange can be an immeasurable blessing, but the web itself is the foundation of existence.

This is why the love affair of Lancelot and Guinevere, Arthur's queen, is so devastating in its consequences. Their sin consists not so much of adultery as of the disordering of their relationships to the Kingdom of Logres. The facts of their position decree that they can love but not become lovers with impunity. When they do become lovers, they pervert their relation to the King and the Kingdom, and because they are among his subjects, they also pervert his relations with all his subjects, and as a result, Logres cannot achieve the Grail. Further, because the web is sundered, the two lovers can no longer love each other. When their relation to the Kingdom disintegrates, they become divided beings: Lancelot a wolf, bestially roaming the forest of Broceliande, and Guinevere like — but how unlike! — Dindrane, in a convent.

Taliessin and Dindrane are also separated, but their separation is the means of their union. They are bound by their mutual love to incarnate Love in the style that is appropriate for them, and neither explicitly nor implicitly does their joint decision to separate constitute a denial of their bodies or a repudiation of sex in their relationship to each other. In fact, they affirm the sexual character of their love precisely by assigning it the role where it will contribute supremely to the web of their loves for each other, the Kingdom of Logres, and God. Bors and Elayne had done the same thing — they had set love in an order appropriate to them — when they married:

the perfect expression of love can be by means of either sexual intercourse or virginity.

According to Christianity, all loves are physical, but sexual interplay is only one of its physical styles, as poetry is only one of the styles of verbal communication. And as the importance and glory of poetry are in no way diminished by recognizing that prose has a valid function, so the depth and power of sexuality are not impugned by recognizing that the body has other organs and functions by which love can be physically expressed. The matter in question is love. The form to be given that matter is a question of style, of which Williams wrote, "possibly what are all problems of style but to find the right kind of motion for the right kind of matter?"

The issue is always between order and chaos, which is to say, between authentic love and any of its myriad of counterfeits, and because order is inherent in love, it can be consummated only if the lovers are obedient to the condition that "Love does not belong to lovers, but they to it". It is this authority of Love over lovers that Taliessin and Dindrane obey when they part. The poem in which they bid farewell to each other does not describe the process by which they had reached that decision; this is done by means of another story which is interwoven with theirs.

A Greek slave-girl is a member of the party escorting Dindrane to the convent, and on the way, the slave is thinking through her own problem of whether to accept the freedom which all slaves in Logres were offered at the end of seven years of servitude, or to remain in Taliessin's household forever, as a slave. In a masterly analysis of the process by which choice is made, Williams shows the steps by which she clears her mind and heart from confusion. The most important of these steps has to do with her desire that Taliessin shall make her decision for her, but this he refuses to do. He exercises his authority over her by compelling her to exercise her own authority. The supreme power of love fosters the independence of other powers: "They can only do it with my lord who can do it without him". Submission to love not only results in freedom; it is the only means by which freedom can be wholly attained, because all other possible lords of our lives — the intellect, the arts, the state, the church, even freedom for its own sake — are ultimately despotic, requiring all subordinate authorities to be subservient to them. Therefore when the slave elects permanent slavery, she is choosing to be free, with all the hazards, responsibilities, and burdens that freedom entails, and she becomes free by electing to submit to the one authority whose service produces authentic freedom.

In another poem, Williams expands this theme by telling how another slave is freed so that she can enter the service of the queen, who will have only free persons around her. After clothing the girl in robes fit for the court, Taliessin seals her liberation by striking her on the face. It is the rite that the Romans used when they released their slaves; it is also an act of contempt, an intensely personal act of rejection. "Henceforth, in the queen's house," Taliessin commands the girl, "be but the nothing We made you, making you something." Freeing her from formal bondage in his household, he confirms her in an infinite service. Raising her from the lowest rank in the social scale, he abases her to a nothing in obedience to love. "At once the blast of union struck her heart." She becomes someone by fully consenting to her nothingness, and the sign of her dismissal is the ratification of her acceptance.

Now, finally, it should be possible to see why, for Williams, the absurdity of life is an excellent absurdity. Love is indeed a foolishness, not because lovers commit follies (although they do), but because to love is freely to exchange, and exchange is the precondition for all life. Our fundamental necessity is the crown of our freedom. Here, as in his supernaturalism, Williams is presenting an alternative to the dominant world views of our day, not a supplement to them. He sees love in the new light of Christianity, rather than in an improved version of the old lights of secularism and paganism. For him, love is only secondarily what the non-Christian declares it to be: a means to human fulfilment and the perfect expression of the real nature of man. Primarily, love *is* reality and reality is love, because existence is dependent upon ordered exchange. Our development, therefore, does not proceed by our first becoming "real persons" and as a result, becoming capable of loving. On the contrary, by our acts of love we slough off all that is insubstantial and illusory in ourselves, and take on substantial existence. And the claim that nothing can be truly known until it is loved, is completed by our apprehension that nothing can be truly loved until it is known, known concretely and carnally with bodily hands and brains and the sturdy acts of the disciplined and liberated imagination.

All man's concerns are rooted in the question of what is real. But he is not able to understand even what this question means until after he has found his answer. He cannot explain why he sets out for Byzantium until he has reached the City and returned from it, and in no case can he justify his journey to those who have never been caught by the rumor of its glory. In his Arthuriad, Williams spreads that rumor in our own time.

# IV

# THE DRAMA OF JUDGEMENT

IN HANDLING QUESTIONS SUCH AS THE NATURE OF THE WORLD, of man, and of God, the creative writer encounters grave problems of content and style, but especially when he is dealing with God or any other ultimate. As Williams wrote in an essay on Milton, "It is very difficult to put Omnipotence and Omniscience into a story, because the proportions of the story are immediately destroyed. In another sense than Cleopatra's, 'The odds is gone.'" God and man are not measurable by the same scale, so that if God or any other ultimate is introduced into a play or picture, man appears as a negligible entity, and if man is made to appear significant, the framework cannot contain God — which is why Williams goes on to say that if the Incarnation had not occurred for the sake of man's redemption, it would have been necessary to invent the doctrine for the sake of his art.

Williams met this difficulty in writing his plays by introducing characters who (like the chorus in classical Greek drama) are not only commentators on the action, but participants in it. The most highly developed of these is the Flame of the Holy Spirit in *The House of the Octopus* (1945), his last three-act play. As with Satan in *The Rite of the Passion* (1931), the Skeleton in *Thomas Cranmer of Canterbury* (1936), the Accuser in *Judgement at Chelmsford* (1939), and their counterparts in some of his one-act plays (as well as the Priest-King in the novel *War in Heaven*), the dominant note of the Flame is irony. "I thought I spoke the truth," laments the repentant priest, and the Flame replies, "I know you did. But then the Faith is much truer than you thought." Cranmer says to Anne Boleyn, "The King is gracious," and the Skeleton interjects, "Heaven is gracious, but few can draw safe deductions on its methods." Seen from above, men are poor, silly things. Worse, they are funny. They struggle so hard, see so dimly, understand so little. Like children, they — we — are so self-important in our small achievements and so crushed by our small failures that it is hard to imagine a God who is genuinely divine who would not find us ridiculous.

There may be some who have never experienced the healing that comes from being laughed at — in love. The contemptuous laugh is destructive and the laughter of comedy is diverting. But do not lover and beloved, at the height of their passion, sometimes break out into laughter at themselves? Do not parents sometimes find their dearly-loved children irresistibly funny? Do we not penetratingly cure ourselves of our dismal pride with laughter? Laughter-in-love restores proportion — but it must be in love, and the kind of love that at once knows the absurdity of the beloved and loves him so much that he will die for him in public shame and lonely agony on a cross. Williams' term for this is "defeated irony", irony that has been double-crossed, as when human absurdity so touches the heart that it intensifies our love for each other, or as when men betray God and send him to his death, and then God betrays his judges and executioners by turning death into a means of grace.

The irony is as real as the discrepancy between the magnitude of man's pretensions and the reality of his finitude and sin. Those who bitterly or scornfully portray man's insignificance and perversion are speaking no more than the truth, and often less than the truth. But the defeat of irony is equally real. We are not worth anyone's love, yet we are loved. We are so wretched and foolish that only a God could love us, but God does love us. The sneering laugh cuts because it contains some truth. The mighty laughter of God makes us whole because it fulfils all truth. He responds to the incongruity between ourselves and him with something still more incongruous. He tops our plaintive story with his own story of covenant, incarnation, and presence.

When Williams depicts the mockery of the Holy Spirit by means of the Flame and his counterparts, he is conclusively dissociating himself from the identification of the Holy Spirit with that alter ego which we call "conscience" or "the inner light". The divine light, he is saying, comes into us from beyond ourselves. It stands opposite to us and opposed to us, thrusting us into intolerable positions, and shredding our old lives so that we are compelled to become new. "The price of heaven or hell or the world is similar," the Skeleton tells Anne Boleyn, " — always a broken heart, sometimes a broken neck." To Cranmer he is even more explicit. "You believe in God; believe also in me; I am the Judas who betrays men to God." And later:

> I am Christ's back; I without face or breath,
> life in death, death in life,
> each a strife with, each a socket for, each,
> in the twisted rear of good will, backward-running speech,
> the derision that issues from doctrines of grace
> through the division man makes between him and his place.
> Christ laughs his foes to scorn, his angels he charges
> with folly; ah, happy who feel how the scorn enlarges!
> I am the thing that lives in the midst of the bones,
> that (seems it) thrives upon moans, the thing with no face
> that spins through the brain on the edge of a spectral voice.

> Rejoice, son of man, rejoice:
> this is the body of Christ which is given for you;
> feed on it in your heart by faith with thanksgiving.

Williams is not referring here to the conflict of man against himself or God, but to the fiercer conflict of God against man. Through the years, much has been said of man's ingrained antagonism to God; in these plays, Williams emphasizes the other stress in the relationship: that God resists us, that he will not allow us to live or die in what we call peace.

Our kind of peace is defined in *The Three Temptations* by Judas, who is there identified with Everyman, when he explains that he is betraying Jesus to obtain peace for mankind: "a little show of goodwill and a quiet future . . . We must wait God's kingdom in a peaceable style and a moderate goodwill . . . I hope I am only thinking of what's best for everyone." But the peace that God offers is not of this kind. It not only passes our understanding; it far overpasses what we anticipate or welcome. Pilate's wife, in the same play, describes it in telling her husband about her dream of Jesus:

> He came to my bed and did not say a word,
> but his face became the face of each of my friends,
> each in turn, each pale, each in its agony,
> each staring at me. I knew their pains,
> the separate secret stubborn pains of each,
> and yet it was no one all the time but he.
> . . . . . . . . . . . . . . . . . .
> I cannot bear my friends' pains; let him go!
> Cannot I love my friends without hurt?
> The sword of his peace pierces me . . .
> . . . is this pain his comfort?
> I cannot bear it; I will not bear it; I must.

The contrast between God's peace and ours has frequently been handled to convey the moral that God's assault on man is "for his own good". It is to Williams' credit that he does not succumb to any of the cheap interpretations of this phrase. If Pilate's wife reaps good from her decision not to armor herself against the sword of the peace of God, this is incidental to the fact that God's will is done in her. The phrase "for your own good" is a superficiality or an evasion in this context, unless the speaker and hearer alike are nakedly conscious that the word "good" almost certainly does not mean, in God, what Everyman wants it to mean.

*The Death of Good Fortune* is directed precisely to this point. Good Luck, in appearance a young nobleman, comes to a certain city, and under his influence the king defeats his enemies; an old woman obtains a house of her own so that she need not live any longer with her daughter-in-law; a lover loves more truly and freely; and a magician sees the fulfilment of his predictions. But neither Good Luck nor those who receive his gifts know who and what he really is. As the Virgin Mary (in this play, the counterpart of the Flame) says, "His nature is heavenly, but when men fell, he was half-blinded", and this is the day that has been appointed for him to discover who he is. While the crowd is worshipping him as a god, he dies — and the king's enemies win a major battle; the old woman loses her house; and the lover doubts his love. Only the magician's daughter, an atheist, is unmoved: she had suspected all along that Good Luck was a fraud. Then Mary calls on Good Luck to rise from the dead. He answers, telling how he is "dying in death", and how he comes to the Christ Child, who takes Luck's heart out of his body, untwists it, and commands him to live. So Luck returns to life with a new name, Blessed Luck, because from the time of the Incarnation when substance became Love and Love substance, *all* luck is good. The old woman and the king cannot believe it. Neither can the magician, but since he knows intellectually that it is true, he ranges himself with the blessing. His daughter and the lover believe while they do not know, and Mary ends the play by saying to them:

> And you, great ones, you must always make your choice,
> or always, at least, know that the choice exists —
> all luck is good — or not; even when the ninth
> step is nine times as difficult as the first.

This is a terrible saying and a terrifying dilemma, and in writing these plays, Williams does not mitigate one shred of the shock they contain. To confront directly the abominable accidents of life (deliberate evil is not in question here) — the mischance that it was *this* man who bought the defective car, *these* women who were passing by when the airplane crashed on the city street, *those* children who lingered after Sunday school on the day the church was bombed — and to say "all luck is good", sounds like the most crass sentimentality, or madness. But Williams also says it in *The House by the Stable,* when Gabriel tells Pride and Hell, "You shall win or lose on the game by the luck of the game, but all luck is good". He says it again in *The House of the Octopus*: "We who have come to our Lord have only to go / farther with our Lord. Everything that can happen / is only to go a little farther with our Lord". And in *The Descent of the Dove,* which is history and not drama, he repeats it by quoting Boethius: "All fortune is good . . . whether be it harsh or be it pleasing . . . yet I know not who would dare to say so to foolish men, for no fool could believe it".

It is Mary and the lovers and the saints who are blessed by the strokes, as well as the caresses, of Holy Luck. As the Flame says, this is "heaven's kind of salvation, not at all to the mind / of any except the redeemed, and to theirs hardly". And "hardly" here means both barely and harshly. The outrages of fortune are not automatically transformed into "the sweetness of fact", and our failure to accomplish this is one of the measures of our distance from God. It is perhaps also a measure of our unwillingness to make the effort and pay the price that he does. We are like that adolescent who, when reminded of how often she had been forewarned that loosening the apron strings is likely to be a painful process, replied through her tears, "Yes, but I didn't realize it was going to *hurt*". He who chooses that all which happens to him shall be used for good and thus be made good is choosing to be crucified, and crucifixion *hurts.* And it is quite possible that it also hurts to be raised from the dead.

Then why do these characters choose crucifixion? One compelling reason is given by the Skeleton, speaking to Cranmer fairly early in his career. "You will choose the rack instead of the cross? I am sorry, friend; it takes longer." A second is suggested by the same quotation: the rack is an instrument for pulling the body apart; it dismembers; it destroys physical integrity. The cross at least does not do that. "He was stretched, He was bled, He was nailed, He was thrust into, but not a bone of Him was broken. The dead wood drenched with the blood, and the dead body shedding blood, have an awful likeness; the frame is doubly saved." On the cross we retain integrity, and few of our natural impulses, if any, are stronger than that which drives us toward integration. Thwarted, it generates anxiety, dread, angst. Fulfilled, it produces a state that is qualitatively so unlike any other, that in the end we are upheld by the framework of the universe even while we are being destroyed within it.

A third reason for choosing the cross instead of the rack is that only in it and on it and by it can laughter be restored without insult to the passion and authenticity of tears. In *The House of the Octopus*, when a South Sea island is invaded by the army of P'o-L'u and its commanding officer orders the little congregation of Christians to pay lip service to its emperor, assuring them that he will understand and even approve their mental reservations, the priest meditates that after all, "the spirit matters more than the letter". The Flame agrees. "Will God dispute over words? no . . .". Then he goes on:

> . . . but man
> must, if words mean anything, stand by words,
> since stand he must; and on earth protest to death
> against what at the same time is a jest in heaven.
> Alas, you are not in heaven! the jests there
> are tragedies on earth . . .

— and to try to have heaven without earth, the celestial comedy without the terrestrial tragedy, is to repeat the primal sin of trying to be as gods.

All Williams' plays are more or less directly concerned with sin and judgement, and consequently with death, heaven, and hell, that appalling trinity of ultimates which we can banish from our thoughts but not from our lives. Modern imaginations tend to associate death with physical corruption, and heaven and hell with medieval representations of burning pits and luminous clouds. They were not very adequate symbols even at the time they were developed, and it is overwhelmingly probable that the artists who used them knew this, as the theologians always have. But ultimate things cannot be discussed at all without symbols in the form of language, analogies with natural phenomena, or extrapolations from common experience. For example, most of us are uncomfortably aware that our choices have consequences that extend farther than we can trace their course, and in directions that we neither intend nor desire. When we come to determine the extent of our ultimate responsibility for these unforeseen and untraceable effects, however, the question immediately arises: How can we talk at all about an *ultimate* responsibility? The traditional style of speaking, not only in Christianity but in most other religions, is in terms of heavens and hells. But whatever description is proposed for these conditions, they are properly understood as declarations that in the last analysis, the limits to our responsibility are not set by ourselves or each other, but are fixed by something or someone beyond ourselves who judges us.

The symbols that Williams chose for discussing these matters may not be any more adequate than the ancient ones, but at least they are different. In *The House of the Octopus,* as in his Arthuriad, hell is the Empire of P'o-L'u. In *Seed of Adam,* hell is Mother Myrrh, who accompanies her son, the Third King, to the nativity of Jesus and is the midwife at his birth. In *The House by the Stable* and *Grab and Grace,* Hell is a man whose twin sister, Pride, is engaged in seducing Man. In *Terror of Light,* hell is the bottom of the sea where the damned creep among the spaces between and under the stones. But whether hell is imaged as a place or a condition or a person, it is immediately available, as heaven also is. We have now the citizenship and the companions we choose, and the judgement of God is a present as well as a future action which reveals not only what we have done, but also what we are now doing while we are persuading ourselves that our motives are consistently high-minded and our actions disinterested.

The reality of this continuing judgement is a major theme in *The House of the Octopus.* Anthony, the missionary priest, is extremely conscientious in fulfilling his double responsibility to protect the integrity of his church, and to convert the pagans who inhabit this island from their cannibalistic religion of "eat or be eaten". Their god consumes his worshippers when they die, unless they have sent him a human sacrifice to be devoured in their stead, and one of the pagans, Assantu, has determined to accomplish this by killing the Christian priest. The curious similarity between these two men becomes apparent when the army of P'o-L'u lands. During the first conversation between the Christians and the invaders, a young Christian girl is frightened into renouncing her faith, and a soldier of P'o-L'u kills her before she can repent.

Anthony had not been present when this happened. When he learns of it, he announces that since she has been an apostate, she is excommunicate, but his deacon and flock reject this judgement.

> She died, even if she lied; she is still a witness.
> Might not, sir, her first baptismal vow
> have swallowed her fault, instead of her fault her vow?
> If God is outside time, is it so certain
> that we know which moments of time count with him,
> and how?

This crisis of interpretation brings on a more serious one, because Anthony cannot bear to lose his control over his congregation. He calls them to return in obedience to him, so that they may enjoy the "peace and fruits of the Spirit". Being named, the Spirit — the Flame — comes, and compels Anthony to answer "as if at the very judgement" the question: "What do you wish?" Anthony replies:

> I would be again
> all that which I was to these once,
> their father, their centre, almost their creator.
> . . . . . . . . . . . .
> I wish you [my people] to spring from me and live from me.
> . . . . . . . . . . .
> I do not wish you to live from God alone;
> I wish always to be your means of God.

Hearing himself speak, he is appalled, but still he insists that the apostate girl is cut off by her own act from the community of the faithful, and he repudiates vehemently the claim of those who saw her die that their faith and bond of love are the stronger because of her martyrdom.

ANTHONY. This is unbelievable and unbearable.
Do you say that this apostate woman and I
are equally profitable to you?

SIRU [the deacon]. Sir, why not?
Thus it becomes us to be her friends and yours,
her children even; she died without children,
but her blood has mothered us in the Faith, as yours fathered.

ANTHONY. This is sheer and absolute lunacy and heresy —

THE FLAME. Assantu will say it better; speak, Assantu.

. . . . . . . . . . .

A fire consumes me;
I must have you for my own, wholly my own, none
shall have you but I. I am the Father, and hungry —

ANTHONY. Jesu God Almighty have mercy upon me!
I do not — I will not — know what I am saying.

THE FLAME. You were praying to my lord the Spirit for exactly that.

Anthony sees himself in Assantu, and repents. In the torments of bitter shame, he forgives the apostate girl whose sin was less than his own, and he is forgiven.

Anthony did not judge himself, but neither was he judged by the Flame of God, or by his flock, or by the faith he professed. His own acts judged him. His thoughts and words and behavior had consequences that redounded upon him according to their nature. He was not condemned for pride and greed; they recoiled upon him as a gun kicks against the shoulder. The only sense in which God judges him is that it is God who decrees that the gun shall recoil, the proud shall perish of their pride, and our responsibilities are not measured solely by our intentions. At the same time, this God has declared that if we choose, he will take the shock of the repercussion upon himself, either directly, or indirectly through one of his creatures who offers himself for this purpose. By the end of the play, Anthony is bearing the girl's sin, and she is bearing his fear of the torture that awaits him at the hands of the headless Emperor of P'o-L'u. The judgement of God is sure and exact, but also it is merciful, because he is willing to suffer the inexorable consequences of evil in the place of those who are directly responsible for it.

This discussion of Williams' plays has become a direct exposition of the doctrines that underlie them. The plays themselves all but compel such an approach. They are images which point to archetypal realities and invoke more than they portray. I am told by persons who are competent to judge that they are good theater; they produce well and have been well received by general audiences. This means that the images — the plays as such — are soundly constructed and captivating, as any image ought to be, and are effective in directing attention to those matters which are their principal concern. In them, form and content are harmoniously joined, no better than in the poems, novels, and essays, but in a very different style. And this difference in style not only sets off Williams' plays from his other work, but sets off his work in all its forms from that of other writers. As Dorothy Sayers has said, "There is scarcely a paragraph in his mature work that could conceivably have been written by anybody else". She was referring explicitly to his literary style; his content, she adds, is original only in the sense that it has been "a source, from which others received the waters of truth", and that "his truth . . . was grounded immutably in its Christian origins". In reading Williams' novels, it is frequently possible to ignore their Christian origin. In reading his poetry, one can sometimes overlook it. But his plays force the readers' attention upon Christian doctrine and tradition with an urgency that is matched only in certain of the essays that constitute the largest proportion of his published work.

# V

# ESSAYS OF EXPLOSIVE CLARITY

GERARD MANLEY HOPKINS ONCE WROTE, "ONE OF TWO KINDS of clearness one should have — either the meaning to be felt without effort as fast as one reads, or else, if dark at first reading, when once made out *to explode.*" And Dorothy Sayers wrote of Charles Williams, "The doctrine was traditional and perennial; his apprehension and presentation of it so individual as at a first encounter to disconcert, perplex, or even antagonise those on whom it did not, on the contrary, break as a sudden light to them that had sat in darkness." If Williams' non-fiction is more explosive and illuminating than his imaginative writings, it is because expository works cannot be brushed off by alluding to fantasies or figures of speech. Or if these works strike the reader less forcibly, it is because they appeal more to the intellect than to the imagination. But every significant point that Williams makes in his imaginative writings is repeated in his critical and discursive works.

Among them are four theological studies, six biographies, four books of literary criticism, and a multitude of smaller pieces: pamphlets, book reviews, articles, editorial introductions, biographical essays, and anthologies. They range in mood from his half-flippant "The One-Eared Man", which describes how a tone-deaf person feels at a concert, to *The Figure of Beatrice,* a full-dress study of Dante's life and work, and from "a history of the Holy Spirit in the Church" to pungent half-column reviews of detective stories. Within these extremes lie the longer reviews on books of poetry, theology, history, anthropology, and an astonishing variety of other subjects, and articles like those on the nature of society and of the body as an image, among them that heart-rending, heart-healing short masterpiece which he contributed to a symposium called *What the Cross Means to Me,* and which has twice been reprinted under the title "The Cross". Even to one who has not read the books that Williams reviewed, most of the reviews themselves are enchanting still, because in them he was likely to be honestly partisan, extending the author's argument or debating hotly with him. Although he used many of these books as springboards for expressing his own opinions, he must often have led the readers of the reviews to the books themselves, in order to get in on the other side of the conversation.

It should not be too surprising that these occasional pieces retain their interest long after the occasion for which they were written has departed. In everything Williams wrote, he related the immediate to the eternal, and eternity, being infinitely contemporaneous, does not go out of date. He did this so consistently and so naturally that a chance remark on almost anything might provoke him to write — for example, a rollicking ballade, strictly correct in form and scribbled as fast as his hand would move — upon its peculiar place in the universe: perhaps only as an occasion for laughter, but that in itself is a grace. "This also is Thou," he kept saying. No event is too trivial, no creature too insignificant to be outside the web of exchange, and since God sustains it there, presumably he has a use for it and we have a responsibility toward it. If nothing else, we can see and point out to others its place in the web. At the same time, he insisted that "This is not Thou": the part does not contain the whole, and the whole cannot be comprehended through any of its parts. Nature as such does not reveal God, even though God can reveal himself through nature, and Beatrice can be for Dante an image of the divine love only because he originally knew her as her very human self.

The formula "This also is Thou; neither is this Thou" is, of course, traditional Christian teaching even though it is not stated in traditional language, and even though the attitude which it encompasses is not commonly practised or understood by Christians. Conservatives will see at once that this is a way of stating the doctrine of the immanence and transcendence of God. Logicians will condemn it for its offence against the rule of identity — that a thing cannot be at once A and not-A. Persons with long memories will be drearily reminded of the representations of the all-seeing eye of God in Victorian parlors. Heresy-hunters will think grim thoughts about Pantheism, Docetism, and Socinianism. And the "God is dead" theologians will properly ignore it, because of Williams' open concern with the unthinkable and all but incredible fact (it was to him a fact) that the Omnipotence has made himself available to man, and therefore all things are suffused with his glory.

Williams seems to have had singularly few delusions about the popularity of this doctrine, or for that matter, about the quality of man's desire for the Kingdom of God, here or hereafter, or for the beatific vision itself. No doubt this skepticism reflected the strength of his belief in original sin, man's innate "preference of an immediately satisfying experience of things to the believed pattern of the universe", which produces as one of its most insidious effects the disinclination to inquire into the ultimate meanings and mysteries of that pattern. Most of us have been taught that our intellects and emotions are fundamentally incompatible, so we let them go their separate ways and endure the consequences of disintegrity believing that they are inherent to the nature of man. In fear or false humility ("Our little minds were never meant . . ."), or ordinary laziness, we do not ask the penetrating questions that would lead to integrity, or we accept the shallow answers that give immediate consolation. Because responsibility implies judgement, we take refuge in the belief that we are not ultimately accountable for our lives, or if we are, that God will let us off with a reprimand. And we succumb to well-meant entreaties that we view the Christian life as "that dreadful thing which you can sometimes smell, the Hearty Adventure of Religion".

"Clear your *mind* of cant," Williams wrote in a review that took the form of a letter to a young friend. Be skeptical of what you have been taught. Be equally suspicious of the demand for immediate relevance and the plea to remain above the battle, of the insistence that the Faith can be rationally justified and the assertion that it exhibits mysteries. Above all, doubt your cherished convictions, and doubt bravely and unceasingly the validity of those misgivings that are the protection and prison of the cowardly in spirit. Our intellects as well as our bodies — and probably more than our bodies —

are infested with sin and permeated with grace. The subtler, more complex structure is open to more influences and capable of greater variations, so that the cold sins of the mind are more abominable than those of the tempestuous and unruly flesh, and not to ask the great questions of life and death, or to ask them only as theoretical puzzles, is to enter upon the way of damnation.

Williams believed that we are free to accept or to reject the Christian world view, but not to evade the choice, because evasion is equivalent to rejection. Therefore, the effect of his writings is to compel a clear cut decision even from those who desire above all else not to decide unequivocally, or not to confess to themselves what decision they have tacitly made. For this reason, his work is characteristically "disturbing". Do we not get along very tolerably without probing relentlessly into such unanswerable problems as "What Is the Meaning of Things?" Is it necessary or wise to take our gaze from the next step in order to descry a problematical distant scene? But Williams is not directing our sight to a future. He is concerned with the God who is here and now, and with the patterns of order and disorder in which we now live. He is not satisfied to live or let live only tolerably well, when a glory is all around us. And he seriously, joyously, passionately believed that a world in which God has become incarnate is irreconcilable with a world which God has never entered to live and die, so that the choice between these worlds is necessarily decisive. Between these two ways of living, these two interpretations of life, there cannot be compromise, and the secular and pagan worlds will always jeer at Christianity because, as Williams said of the Fool of the Tarot, "man finds it folly till it is known. It is sovereign or it is nothing, and if it is nothing then man was born dead". "All luck is good — or not."

In our time, we cannot easily avoid inquiring into the present and future importance of Williams' body of work. This question has not always been as pressing for writer or reader as it is now, when value is generally understood to reside in historical fame or instantaneous impact, rather than in correspondence with reality. If — as some voices tell us — the language hitherto employed for speaking of ultimate matters has become irretrievably alien, so that words like sin and forgiveness, or God and Redeemer, must be abandoned by any who wish to be heard by "modern" man, Williams' influence will soon be lost. He used these words and others that are still more offensive, like Holy Trinity, incarnation, salvation, and holiness. His categories of thought were equally traditional, so if Christianity does free itself from these residues of its history, Williams' writings will go into the discard with them.

There is, however, the possibility that these words have become vacuous because we have carelessly or fearfully adjusted the concepts to our immediate desires, instead of growing up into them. The idea of "estrangement", for example, which is often used as a synonym for "sin", is comparatively easy to live with because it does not carry the quality of outrage that the Christian has traditionally assigned to sin. And the popular interpretation of the statement, "God is the ground of being", has in it little or nothing of the force and initiative, or the peril to ourselves, of "the Omnipotent God". If Christianity is deeply true, however, we will discover in our lives that only the ancient categories of thought, and the words like hope and absolution and love that designate them, are rich enough in either connotation or intensity to reflect the quality of our living. And there are now a good many people, both Christians and non-Christians, who have seen in their own lives enough of the glory that Williams defines, that they turn to him again and again for sustenance, without regard for the neglect, opposition, or acclaim of literary and theological critics.

Williams' particular genius was for imagery, which is an indirect approach and has a delayed-action fuse. If he had used this method to communicate familiar and accepted ideas, he probably would have been noticed briefly as a stylist and forgotten. But he was speaking to a world that does not know Christianity, or that has become bored with it, or knows only its superficial features. To this world, he had something fresh to say and he said it in a fresh style, thereby creating confusion for those who could not disentangle the substance of his thought from its form, and antagonizing those who reject his world view, as well as those who simply dislike imagery as such. At the same time and in the same words, he has disclosed to some readers a new world and a new life, with an explosion of clarity accompanied not by the heat of a nuclear disintegration, but by the sudden warmth of spring.

## SELECTED BIBLIOGRAPHY

This list includes only those books which in my opinion are of widest interest and (with two exceptions in the field of literary criticism) are currently in print. Most of these are available in more than one edition; I give here the one that is likely to be most accessible to the American reader. So far as I can discover, no definitive bibliography of Charles Williams' work has been published. The most extensive is in my book on his theology, which should be supplemented with Lawrence R. Dawson, Jr.'s checklist of Williams' book reviews.

NOVELS — in the order I usually recommend for reading them. Except where otherwise noted, all are published in paperback by Wm. B. Eerdmans Publishing Co., Grand Rapids, Michigan, 1965.

1. *Many Dimensions, War in Heaven, Descent into Hell.*
2. *All Hallows' Eve* (New York: Noonday Press), *The Place of the Lion, The Greater Trumps* (New York: Noonday Press).
3. *Shadows of Ecstasy.*

ARTHURIAN POETRY. I strongly recommend that the individual poems be read in the order proposed by C. S. Lewis in *Arthurian Torso,* and unless the reader is thoroughly grounded in the Arthurian legend, that he also follow Lewis' commentary as he proceeds.

*Taliessin through Logres* and *The Region of the Summer Stars* (one volume). London: Oxford University Press, 1948.

*Arthurian Torso.* Containing the Posthumous Fragment of the Figure of Arthur by Charles Williams and a Commentary on the Arthurian Poems of Charles Williams by C. S. Lewis. London: Oxford University Press, 1947.

PLAYS

*Collected Plays by Charles Williams.* Edited by John Heath-Stubbs. London: Oxford University Press, 1963.

THEOLOGICAL WORKS

*He Came Down from Heaven* and *The Forgiveness of Sins* (one volume). London: Faber & Faber, 1938.

*The Descent of the Dove*: a History of the Holy Spirit in the Church. (Faber & Faber, 1939). Grand Rapids: Wm. B. Eerdmans Publishing Co., 1965.

*Witchcraft.* (Faber & Faber, 1941). New York: Meridian Books, 1959.

ARTICLES AND REVIEWS

*The Image of the City and Other Essays.* Edited and with an Introduction by Anne Ridler. London: Oxford University Press, 1958.

*Selected Essays.* Edited by Anne Ridler. London: Oxford University Press, 1961.

LITERARY CRITICISM

*The Figure of Beatrice*: a Study in Dante. (Faber & Faber, 1943). New York: Noonday Press, 1961.

*The English Poetic Mind.* London: Oxford University Press, 1932.

*Reason and Beauty in the Poetic Mind.* London: Oxford University Press, 1933.

MATERIAL ABOUT CHARLES WILLIAMS — chosen to give a wide range of critical opinion. Items that are starred contain important biographical information.

W. H. Auden, "Charles Williams: a Review Article". *The Christian Century,* Vol. LXXIII, No. 18, May 2, 1956, pp. 552-554.

Robert McAfee Brown, "Charles Williams: Lay Theologian". *Theology Today,* Vol. X, No. 2, July 1953, pp. 212-229.

Glen Cavaliero, "The Way of Affirmation". *The Church Quarterly Review,* January-March 1956, pp. 19-28.

Robert Conquest, "The Art of the Enemy". *Essays in Criticism,* Vol. 7, No. 1, January 1957, pp. 42-55; plus the correspondence that followed: *Ibid.,* No. 3, July 1957, pp. 330-343.

Lawrence R. Dawson, Jr., "A Checklist of Reviews by Charles Williams". *Papers of the Bibliographical Society of America,* Vol. 55, Second Quarter 1961, pp. 110-117.

————. "Reflections of Charles Williams on Fiction". *Ball State Teachers College Forum,* Vol. V, No. 1, Winter 1964, pp. 23-29.

*T. S. Eliot, "The Significance of Charles Williams". *The Listener,* Vol. XXXVI, No. 936, 19 December 1946, pp. 894-895.

George Every, S.S.M., "Charles Williams—I. The Accuser". *Theology,* Vol. LI, No. 333, March 1948, pp. 95-100; and "II—The City and the Substitutions", *Ibid.,* No. 334, April 1948, pp. 145-150.

————. *Poetry and Personal Responsibility.* London: SCM Press, Ltd., 1949, chapters I and IV.

*Alice Mary Hadfield, *An Introduction to Charles Williams.* London: Robert Hale Ltd., 1959.

H. D. Hanshell, "Charles Williams: A Heresy Hunt". *The Month,* New Series, Vol. 9, No. 1, January 1953, pp. 14-25.

John Heath-Stubbs, *Charles Williams.* London: Published for The British Council by Longmans, Green & Co., 1955.

F. R. Leavis, *The Common Pursuit.* London: Chatto & Windus, 1952, pp. 252ff.

*C. S. Lewis, Introduction to *Essays Presented to Charles Williams.* (Oxford, 1947). Grand Rapids, Mich.: Wm. B. Eerdmans Publishing Co., 1966.

Geoffrey Parsons, "The Spirit of Charles Williams". *The Atlantic Monthly,* Vol. 184, No. 5, November 1949, pp. 77-79.

John Press, *The Chequer'd Shade.* London: Oxford University Press, 1958, pp. 59-61.

*Anne Ridler, Introduction to *The Image of the City and Other Essays.* London: Oxford University Press, 1958.

Dorothy L. Sayers, Introduction to *James I* by Charles Williams. London: Arthur Barker Ltd., 1934.

Mary McDermott Shideler, *The Theology of Romantic Love*: A Study in the Writings of Charles Williams. (Harper, 1962). Grand Rapids, Mich.: Wm. B. Eerdmans Publishing Co., 1966.

Barbara Ward, Review of Charles Williams' *The Figure of Beatrice. The Dublin Review,* Vol. CCXIV, 1944.

*Michal (Mrs. Charles) Williams, "As I Remember Charles Williams". *Episcopal Churchnews,* Vol. CXIX, No. 14, April 12, 1953, pp. 12-14.

Elizabeth Wright, "Theology in the Novels of Charles Williams". *Stanford University Honors Essays in Humanities,* No. VI, 1962.